THE WILD SPII

SAM ALLEN

Copyright ©2022 Sam Allen. All Rights Reserved.

No part of this publication may be reproduced, distributed, or transmitted in any form or by any means, including photocopying, recording or other electronic or mechanical methods, or by any information storage and retrieval system without the prior written permission of the author/publisher, except in the case of very brief quotations embodied in critical reviews and certain other non-commercial items permitted by copyright law.

CONTENT WARNING: This book contains erotic themes which may be offensive to some readers and/or inappropriate for children. Reader discretion is advised.

Cover art by Klaudia Kindler

To discover more of Sam's poetry, be sure to visit her blog:

www.peacockpoetryblog.wordpress.com

TABLE OF CONTENTS

TABLE OF CONTENTS 2
WHY I WROTE THIS BOOK 3
ACKNOWLEDGMENTS 5
THE POEMS 11
TRUTH 12
FREEDOM 32
FIRE 53
PLEASURE 62
SELF-LOVE 91
LOVE 112
LIVE POETRY 150
MORE ABOUT ME 151
BEFORE YOU GO 153

WHY I WROTE THIS BOOK

Four years ago a door slammed shut and my life changed dramatically. Whilst shocking at the time, in retrospect this was the biggest universal kick-up-the-bum that I have ever received! Just as I said goodbye to a hugely significant chapter in my life, I was struck by a synchronous and life-changing experience.

One sunny early summer afternoon, a random lady on a bus made eye contact with me and struck up a conversation and seemed to think that we knew each other somehow. This approach was in itself unusual, given the fact that Swiss culture tends to be quite private and reserved.

The curious stranger asked me if I was musical and then, as we exited the bus at the same stop, invited me to come and see her apartment. Something told me to follow her unexpected impulse and on entering the small apartment, we exchanged a few pleasantries and she then directed my eyes to one side of the room.

Upon the wall there was a large, red, textured, sultry painting with the words "Der Wille" (will or intention) written boldly above it. In that very moment, my whole Being knew exactly what was being communicated. This was the most powerful sense of calling forth that I had ever experienced. I was receiving an undeniable sign that a divine path was opening up before me and I knew instantaneously that my new journey was about reclaiming my wild, feminine spirit. I was being called to feel, own and fully express my fiery passion. To live my desire. To take giant leaps on that eternal human journey towards greater authenticity and self-love.

And so I am. With full permission. Unapologetically.

This poetry book is for you if you identify with and/or have an interest in the expression of the wild, feminine spirit.

The intention for this book is to share some of the poems that have helped me to evoke the many colours of my own femininity. Poetry that has helped me to connect more deeply to **Truth**, **Freedom, Fire**, **Pleasure**, **Self-Love** and **Love** and to process my joy and my grief in the most cathartic of ways.

Wild can be anything you want it to be.

I hope that by sharing my poetry both in written and in live recital form, I can encourage you to access and liberate your feminine power. To give it a voice. To dance with it. To savour it. To flirt with it. To create from it. To honour its vulnerability and to celebrate its strength.

Yes, you!

With Wild Love,

Sam

ACKNOWLEDGMENTS

Special thanks to the following special souls and cheerleaders, many of whom have been encouraging me to publish a poetry book for years! I'm blessed to know you.

Andy - My Earth, my home, my grounding force. I love you deeply. You teach me that love is a verb. Every day. My best friend and adored Crazy Cat Dad.

Ziggy, Ebony and Nera - Our three cats who show me how to be wild, playful and free.

Mum - For raising me to be quirky, open-minded and fun-loving through your own example.

Migena - For being my much-loved, loving, playful, caring, untamed DynamiX, podcasting co-creatrix and dear, dear friend who knows me inside out.

My Eccentric Sisters, Liz, Sparkles and Genius - Who love and understand me however I am and allow my craziness to express itself as it so desires. I feel so held by you.

Donatella - My kindred spirit and soul Home on earth. For the power of your gentleness. For truly seeing me. For the healing we evoke in each other and for the knowing that we were always meant to meet.

My Iguanas - My place of belonging. My tribe. You have taught me the true meaning of Staying.

Petra - For awakening me to my Shakti energy, my personal power and so much more. For helping me to channel my energy in nourishing and exciting ways. I learn so much from you! You inspire me.

Lluís-Marc - For your tender-hearted masculinity. And your love of humanity. It is an honour to know you dear Brother.

Elaine - For embodying grounded Fire and showing how it's done.

Helena - For your wisdom and spiritual guidance. And for being able to simply Be with you in whichever place I'm in.

Gail - My fellow passionate Aries sister, a genuine friend and for being the reason that I ended up making Switzerland my home.

Isabelle - For your honesty, empathy, realness, unwavering friendship and love.

Sari - For our joyful, effortless energetic and spirited connection and soulful conversations.

Zuzana - For being a fun-loving, faithful and fabulous friend who arrived just at the right time. So grateful for you.

Caro - For being such a playful, loving, generous and open companion on this journey of conscious sexuality.

Gail CS - For your solidarity, sensitivity and friendship.

Michelle - For encouraging me to have difficult conversations for the sake of personal growth.

MJ - For calling forth my self-expression and naming what you saw in me just when it mattered.

Klaudia – for the beautiful book cover design.

Ronnie - For your rock-solid mentoring support throughout my Leadership journey. I was touched by your willingness to be there for me.

Ursula - For honouring the poet in me and inviting me to celebrate my creativity.

Anne - For beautiful readings, blessings and truly understanding high sensitivity.

Emma - For your insatiable sense of adventure, your realness and your warmth.

Afsheen - For your absolute belief in me and for your strength of character and sense of fairness. You're incredible.

Kezza - For loving me and accepting me warts-and-all since the day we met back in Rownhams Primary School!

Gazza - For being a great friend to me through those formative UKC days and beyond.

Tina - For being there. In timeless ways. I trust you implicitly. You're a vault.

Joukje - For getting it. Always. And for your generous, spacious presence and pure charm.

Dani - For having faith in me.

Francine - For being my French Mum for the year. And for making me feel loved.

Rownhams Girls - For over 40 years of unconditional friendship.

Andreja, Lena, Regina and Aje - For the safe haven of our weekly coaching exchange and our mutual support.

Dornach Gospel Choir - For the spiritual solidarity of singing together and for making me feel so welcome.

Tiffany – For your inspiring commitment to personal transformation and for your incredible artwork.

George – for those wonderful visualisations and for holding great space for my creativity.

Cosmin – for helping my inner child to heal and for your warmth and humanity.

To my amazing clients – For your courage, openness and trust.

To my Phoenix colleagues – Together we rise stronger.

Auntie Glen - For modelling what it is to live with resilience, humour and your heart-on-your-sleeve.

Grandma – For your pure love.

Brian - for helping me to finally get my book out there. And for your unending patience.

And to my dear Dad - For showing me how to love with all my heart and to have complete reverence for this gift called life. For your humility. For allowing me to see what being a really decent human being looks like. For your fortitude. You inspire me to create every day. You taught me how to give voice to my emotions. You taught me that pure joy that can be found in creative expression. You lit up every room that you entered, dear Dad. I am eternally grateful for your almighty presence and I am so blessed to have had you as my guide. I love you more than words could ever say.

THE POEMS

TRUTH

Eye of the Beholder

Your truth's what makes you beautiful

Which story are you telling?

The real and not the dutiful

is what makes you compelling

Your voice is such an instrument

May your words be authentic

For when you are in synch with them

They'll feel how much you meant it

We don't need to gloss over it

We don't need to restrain it

Your life you are the boss of it

Your message - do not tame it

For who you are's immutable

It's time to start rebelling

Your truth's what makes you beautiful

Which story are you telling?

Phoenix

I am the Phoenix that frees up the Truth

A rise-from-the-fire style lesson

I am the courage that helps you to choose

to speak from your heart-centred essence

Calling you forth, I'm your shimmering North

From the fall there is great elevation

I am the pure and resilient force

for what's felt is our greatest salvation

I am the Trust that my soul is renewed

I give voice to the source of my presence

I am the Phoenix that frees up the Truth

A rise-from-the-fire style lesson

What Counts

The stars are all that matter

The plough, the moon, your dreams

Those harmless daily natters

The softly flowing stream

Your ego can misguide you

Duped by the weight of thought

But when you look outside, you

will find the truth you've sought

And when your life's in tatters

You've more than it might seem

The stars are all that matter

The plough, the moon, your dreams

Passion's Journey

I walked on rocky, wild terrain

I walked through thunderstorms and rain

No man my walking could restrain

I walked through fear and doubt and pain

The sun resurfaced on the plain

I took a break, then walked again

My barefoot spirit did not wane

The walk was always worth the gain

Abstain from walking I could not

It was my path, it was my lot

It shook my tension, freed my knots

Like chains, to stand still in one spot

I trudged through mud and wet marshland

My soles alight, I walked through sand

In need of water, my feet blistered

Hungry, tired, ankle twisted

Somehow still I kept on going

When I would stop, no way of knowing

The miles stretched on, the ground was dry

I saw exhaustion in the sky

Like empty lungs, the clouds did sag

But this was not yet in the bag

I climbed up rocks and mountain peaks

Through movement our emotions speak

I hiked through valleys, lush and breathing

Pushed through anger, red soul seething

Wandered, silent, introspection

Earth's raw beauty, deep affection

Until my being had expressed

The passion in its every step

Cross-legged I sat still and smiled

The walking had all been worthwhile

THINGS I CANNOT BE WITH

Over-seriousness

Busy roads with no proper pavements

Too much small talk

The word "cool" when used as an attribute to aspire to

People that fact me off

Fickleness

Superficiality

Blatantly opportunistic behaviour

Complacency

Overt judgement

The feeling of being silently judged

Sycophants

Ordering fish in a restaurant and discovering I have to filet it myself

Being in buildings for too long

Homophobia

Any phobia based on rejecting a minority due to their supposed non-conforming to a social norm

Noisy evenings

People who assume they know more without asking

Black ice

Being in busy airport gate check-in queues

Being static

Being told what I'm thinking or feeling

Bitchiness

Glass half-emptiness

Maps

People who assume all women are good in the kitchen. Or should be. Or even want to be.

Saying goodbye to people I love

Competitiveness

Violence

The smell of Cointreau (don't ask!)

One-way conversations

People who have loud mobile phone conversations on public transport

Hypocrisy

Fakeness

Waves

Sometimes they drift in with no sign

My eyes they sting with salty brine

And sometimes they float over me

And cleanse me of uncertainty

Sometimes they crash onto my shore

And almost knock me to the floor

Their force and magnitude so strong

My soul is simply swept along

Sometimes they lap onto the sand

I walk beside them, hand in hand

But then one sneaks up from behind

I feel I'm drowning in my mind

The timing of these waves is strange

They always make me grow and change

As they wash in I understand

We are but tiny grains of sand

Upon a universal beach

I'm open to what my waves teach

Relentless

Thrash me hard into the walls against the storm raged pier

Smash me down, I'll take it all, and still I'll reappear

Scrape my legs against the rocks, push my head in the sand

My soul has seen a thousand knocks, each time I fall, I stand

Engulf me with your reckless waves, drop me from seagull's height

You'll see with time that I won't cave, I'll still get up and fight

Rock my boat, deflate my sails, reduce my bones to dust

The passion in my heart won't pale, nor will my Truth or Trust

For life is precious and immense, each breath a brand-new start

and Love is all that can make sense to my wide, hungry heart

Wash me up into the bay, exhausted and confused

For I'll come back in my own way - it's Yes to Life, I choose

Poetic Pact

I write each morning without fail

Whichever state or mood prevails

At home, abroad, laid in my bed

When I don't know, I write instead

Upon a bench, among the trees

Inside my lounge, beside the sea

Each setting can be poetry

When I observe it lovingly

When I am up or down I write

Don't try too hard, I just invite

the words to tumble through my pen

A habit started way back when

I lost my hero of a Dad

and I felt so profoundly sad

Received a message strong and clear

to write things down, and rhyme appeared!

I made a pact that come what may

From then on I'd write every day

I write for fun, for liberation

Each day begins with pure creation

If I feel blocked, if I have doubts

Then this too I can write about!

It's how my soul communicates

It brings me home to contemplate

I write to share, I write to heal

I write whatever my heart feels

I do not seek to be a buff

Or write intelligent sounding stuff

(Though this I can do very well)

For me expression much more tells

I'm like a kid with a new toy!

I write because it brings me joy

For seven years I've written now

Some simple lines, and some that wow

Wherever I am on life's trail

I write each morning without fail

Ruth

Road Stop Café, late July

Slumped down into her chair

Her eyes all smudged, her thoughts awry

Jet black, her long thin hair

A piercing on her subtle nose

Her arms, a tattooed mess

The stamps of old loves I supposed

Hard to let go I guess

Sewn in her brow, some bitterness

Betrayal and some lies

Yet still a faint hope etched within

The crow's feet around her eyes

She held herself with heaviness

No one would dare go near

And guarded like it was her young

Her lukewarm pint of beer

It was as if she'd lived her life

Her mouth a tired pout

Though she was barely forty-one

She now was all rocked out

Road Stop Café, late July

I'll never know her truth

But I could feel her inner cry

Upon her necklace "Ruth"

Embracing Eccentricity

It's quirkiness that makes me tick

Don't do polished, don't do slick

Prefer to sparkle on my own

Don't want to be a mindless clone

Don't want to follow like a sheep

And walk through my life half-asleep

It's truth and beauty that I seek

And my life's purpose is unique

And if my choices are offbeat

Move over, take a different seat

Cause I want more out of this life

Than playing the adoring wife

Don't have fun comparing houses

Don't care what car that your spouse has

Don't aspire to be famous

Not some kind of ignoramus

Have a deep emotional well

A blessing and a curse as well

But it's these feelings when expressed

That make me stand out from the rest

Because they're powerful and strong

Unleashing them helps me belong

You might call me a throwback hippie

But not so high and not so dippy

Avoiding all duplicity

Embracing eccentricity

Cerulean Sonnet

My love affair with blue, where does one start?

You've stilled the starkest storms with languid look

And taken residence within my heart

And turned my fiery eyes into bright brook

The coolness of your stance cannot be stirred

You've blurred the black with soothing turquoise ease

For now your true contentment I have heard

Calm words of peaceful poise my mind appease

But glassy you may be, I can't see through

Your depth I am inept to reach below

Whence your repose sprang forth, I have no clue

Enigma of disguise, what drives your flow?

Though mystery exudes from calmest lake

I'm closer to my truth, make no mistake

Truth Telling

Speaking truth empowers us

It sets our hearts in motion

What we repress devours us

Give voice to your emotion

When we play parts, we cannot grow

Our souls are in stagnation

When we let go, let our words flow

There's healing liberation

To show up as we truly are

deep down, can be contagious

So let your presence set the bar

Be open and courageous

For what we hold back sours us

Free love, you've my devotion

Yes speaking truth empowers us

It sets our hearts in motion

Source

You speak to me in vibrant violets that beam through cracked path

You come to me through the inner knowingness of an awakening that I do not yet fully understand

Just yesterday in fact you landed as a flamboyant red butterfly

resting teasingly before my feet as a reminder of the lightness

of transformation

One day you even crawled towards me across the stony street in salamander form,

your flash siren markings confounding

my connection to an undeniable

psychic sensitivity

This morning I watch you bobbing, effortlessly in the air like a baby-blue balloon,

my right hand holding your preciously delicate string of connection

A grounding cord.

There is a slow-motion sense of serenity as I gaze,

transfixed by the grace of your harmonious motion

You speak to me through the goodness of his loving voice, infusing my soul with constant validation

It's funny. When the supposed luxury of choice is removed from this world

It is amazing what we are able to see.

The phoniness no longer has a place.

And from here:

I come into my own!

FREEDOM

Choose Life

Each day is different from the last

Embrace the now, forget the past

Don't ruminate, don't second guess

Appreciate your every breath

For you are cherished, you are blessed

You matter just as do the rest

Your hungry heart, your crazy ways

A vital part of this life play

You are a gem, you're here to shine

Sometimes there's mess, sometimes you're fine

Roll up your sleeves and have a blast

Each day is different from the last

MADRID

This was a heat like I had never experienced before.

A thick, steamy blanket of infernal intensity that forced you into the present

like a volcanic ultimatum.

There were people passing out on buses

salsa dancing around the midnight streets

living the nocturnal hours

as if the day had just broken

I was intimidated

enthralled

and acclimatising

My rosy English demeanour struggling to compose itself

amidst the assured merriment

of this urban fiesta

Too much traffic

Too many people

Too much noise

and it excited and invaded my soul simultaneously

As I gaze at the photo captured earlier that evening, I remember the burning, bitter kick of

unfiltered coffee.

I see myself posing in that darkened room

with my intensity

my insecurity

and my natural curiosity

and I soften.

That free-spirited Euro adventurer

with a creative heart and a precarious passion

for the unknown

is still

so present.

She is a wild and sensitive girl who needs me to free her and keep her protected

in equal measures.

And we are getting there.

Rugged Source Bay

I'm flying down the Heartfelt Highway

Loose hair flapping in the wind

The feeling I can do this my way

Mischievously makes me grin

Can hardly hold back my elation

Soon the waves won't be restrained

My heart thumps with anticipation

Nothing ventured, nothing gained

This is my place, this is my mission

My adventure and my day

My open heart without condition

Full and free at Rugged Source Bay

I am the weathered wild rock setting

I am the tousled, turning tide

I love the green light my soul's getting

Seaspray stirs me deep inside

I am the restless, blooming dune rose

I'm in the raucous seagulls' cry

I'm more myself each time the wind blows

Thrilling life shines from my eyes

Mystic Messenger

You flew into the window frame

All fragile, red and frantic

Your powdered wings now limp and strained

From your resistant antics

I cupped my hand and helped you land

upon a place more stable

until the scent of freedom fanned

and your wings were enabled

As off you sped, my mind you led

into more transformation

To gently coax oneself instead

of forcing, frees creation

I think you knew, that's why you came

For nature is my teacher

You flew into the window frame

Oh fleeting red-winged creature

WIDER TRUST

It doesn't help at all to cling

to places, people, time and things

For life is change, some moments pass

Not everything that's good can last

When we let go, we create space

What's new begins to take its place

The seasons shift, the old dissolves

The universe upgrades our soul

It doesn't help when we resist

or try to force back what we miss

What's meant for us will always be

Divinely timed and perfectly

The wanting, wishing and the longing

to other time frames now belonging

"Accept the here and now, don't cling"

(is what my soul to my heart sings)

"Love all those people, places, things

and set them free, expand your wings"

Viola's Rebellion

Her face is white as porcelain

Her lips are thin and red

And as the concertina plays

He tilts her fragile head

The voice that he embodies

Has a churlish, silly sound

He helps her do a courtesy

And then makes her spin around

Her floral dress, conservative

Her frilly blouse too tight

Those fallen locks have lost their shine

But who is she to fight?

She's at the mercy of his hands

She doesn't have control

The only life she's ever known

Is as a passive doll

She's tired of the girlishness

The way he moves her hands

She hates the curtseys and the nods

The way he makes her stand

And suddenly as if possessed

Viola takes her reins

Decides to pull on her own strings

And breaks free from her chains

She smiles a smile so devilish

It almost cracks her cheeks

Does a crazy, happy dance

And turns to him to speak

She tells him with authority

That it's time for a change

She's had enough of mannerisms

Feeling so restrained

Viola takes a flying leap

And breaks her string of pearls

Shouts that she's a woman now

And not some helpless girl

She tears her frilly blouse apart

Her hair is like a horse

Cascading down her ivory skin

With such unbridled force

Her pearls are swirling round the sky

That floral skirt is ripped

She steps into her own domain

And swings her sensual hips

She turns to the ventriloquist

Who stands there quite aghast

Thanks him for the life she's had

But adds, "It couldn't last.

Inside each doll there is a soul

That longs for more than pity,

We women want to be ourselves

It's boring playing pretty"

Viola so vivaciously

Vibrates with violet power

She's waited all her life for this

It is her finest hour

She spins him once and twice around

And takes her fallen laces

Ties his hands and feet with them

She laughs as her heart races

Viola's purple passion pumps

Right through her female brain

"Cause even dolls rebel you know,

And now I hold the reigns"

Note from my 18-Year-old Self

I didn't vanish into thin air

when you cut my wild locks and squeezed me into that tight wooden box

Did you not hear the desperate banging woman?

My carefree, fantastical, pink-blossom heart thumping at your dampened-down adult's door

begging you for attention?

Now finally you give me some airspace, and I'm going to take it all!

What I want is:

To tumble down your shoulders in a beautifully dishevelled mane of magic

To spend slow-mo days dreaming of my soul's desire whilst bathing in the forest's love

To hug close friends and trees and to quench my colossal thirst for touch and affection

For us to play together and experiment in ways that you have long forgotten

To feel like no matter what happens you will keep me safe and warm and well

Your undivided love and attention

I am your Freedom

and your Abandonment

and your Purity

I am an incorrigible Dreamer

I am fragile and fearless and quirky and quite unforgettable

and I need you, you know

just as you need me

and my

Truth

Wild Wave

I'm the wild wave that rides with the tide

My zest is the crest of the breakers

Surfing upon the emotions inside

For I'm a born liberty maker

Joyful and free with the thought I can be

anything that my spirit is wishing

Kindred of choice, I'm a deep open sea

and in turn I give others permission

Leaping and loving and spurting with pride

My aliveness can be a soul-shaker

I'm the wild wave that rides with the tide

My zest is the crest of the breakers

Primitivity

The strength that rises from the ground draws up into my centre

It makes a deep and tribal sound, calls forth my wild inventor

There is great weight and in this state my heart casts strong vibrations

I don't react to jibes and baits, there's no deliberation

Bring on the urge, the cleanse, the purge, the thump of feelings ardent

I am not sentences and words, do not explain or pardon

What I've been dealt is sensed and felt, it shakes through my whole system

My thinking self begins to melt as with my soul I listen

We keep ourselves so tightly wound, allow Earth's source to enter

Invite the strength deep in the ground and move from your raw centre

LEAP OF FAITH

I plunge into the open

Each inch of me alive

Propelled by heart and hoping

This is my soul's skydive

Reacting not deflecting

Impactful and immense

There's nothing worth protecting

where logic makes no sense

This moment is my mission

I stretch out to the max

My parachute; permission

I burst out through the cracks

There's wonderment around me

I span the endless sky

The rightfulness dumbfounds me

At height there is no I

Expanded and empowered

By love and life and grace

My confidence a tower

This is my leap of faith

THE TEPEE TIMES

The Tepee Times were legendary

We burned our bras that night

And tied them up triumphantly

The branches stayed upright

There had been trying times for us

But we had found each other

Like hippies from a magic bus

With two new Belgian lovers

In Harbledown we made our pitch

Lit candles round our tent

We laughed and cried, a touch bewitched

Beneath the moon we'd vent

And Legend captured everything

We were indoctrinated

Bob Marley made our troubles sing

A fine friendship created

Although we are a world apart

Life sent our paths diverting

The Tepee Times stay in my heart

No one could try subverting

THANKING TRAUMA (OTTAVA RIMA)

The day they let me go it all began

You were the most unlikely kind of friend

My heart's desire was buried under sand

And you put my containment to an end

A blessing in disguise, I understand

For we attract the longings that we send

And thanks to you I'm more myself each day

You cleared the reasons not to from my way

Confusing though it was, somehow I knew

I'd walk beyond the chaos into Light

You cast me on this path so I'd breakthrough

into an incarnation that felt right

Perceptive one, yes you turned up on cue

I grew so much throughout those sleepless nights

It's those who can withstand who face the test

For dreams in unknown ways may manifest

FIRE

FURESCALA

Furescala, the flame thrower

She once got badly burned

She lay down on the kitchen floor

All alone and spurned

Scalded by the heat of love

Consumed by her desire

Furescala felt powerless

But learned to trust her fire

Harnessing the energy

And no longer forlorn

Hell it knows no fury

Like a woman scorned

A blazing, burning rhapsody

So powerful and bold

Seething through her very core

And how her flames could scald

She flipped the anger inside out

And turned it on its head

Flaming, fierce and passionate

Her heart was strong and red

Spicy, hot, like chilli seeds

And thumping with such ire

Instead of holding it inside

She set her soul on fire

She sang it and she painted it

She danced it, celebrated

Instead of letting it consume her

She simply created

Furescala was furious

And she had flames to throw

And once she'd fully felt her rage

She smiled and let it go

CREATIVE FIRE

It's how I'm made, it's how I'm wired

My soul is a Creative Fire

Come from the raw, the heat, the mess

I burn inside when unexpressed

The flames invoke, the flames speak truth

What's pure can never be uncouth

I'm full-on passion, turned on heat

and I march to my own damn beat

I chase the light, embrace the dark

Dynamic, vibrant, full of spark

When I hold back, there is implosion

My natural state is: Free Explosion!

Magnetic when my furnace roars

Glow on is what my blaze implores

I'm here to feel, confess, ignite

To dare to speak of what excites

In full permission, dancing higher

My soul is a Creative Fire

Dynamic Heart

Pumping through the wilderness of dry bones

and wasteland

It beats on, anon

The scarlet scales of passion

scaling through her body

with indomitable will

Thriving through the thickness of terse words

and lacerating labels

Onwards and upwards

Gliding across rough rapids and coarse stone

Beating with bountiful barrels of sentient spirit

A fervent fist of faith and fortitude

Lifting and lighting her upturned universe with the healing hammer of hope

Of course she had it in her.

She,

The Dynamic Heart.

JUST WRITE

Just write and let your soul take flight

Let undiscovered sparks ignite

On wakeful, starry lonesome nights

Let your pen run amok and write

Let dark blue ink run down your page

Uncork your deep red wine that's aged

Release your truth, creative sage

How lions roar when they're uncaged!

Just write with no end goal in sight

Transmit your very human plight

The grammar police are sleeping tight!

Within your fingers there is light

Just write, express with all your might

Fear not of being wrong or right

Your heart's desire, your inner fight

Paint what you feel with words, just write!

DANCING WITH FIRE

I want to slow dance in your arms

I want you to seduce me

To hold me in your warming calm

I want you to unloose me

It's not about that someone else

The heat is there within you

I want you into me to melt

I want to feel your sinews

I feel the way your body aches

I feel the hollow missing

I want to make your body shake

To send your soul-space hissing

For you're the one snake I can't charm

Come let your flames infuse me

I want to slow dance in your arms

I want you to seduce me

The Passion Chant

I am the flames of love within your loins

I am the swirling vortex of your soul

I am the raging drama of your heart

I am the force that helps you come alive

I am the twinkle in your hungry eyes

I am the maker of your inner dreams

I am the broody, sultry, stormy sky

I am the way your hair looks when unbrushed

I am the racing charge of your wild mind

I am the place you go when you've no map

I am destructive when I'm kept inside

I am the very food you feast upon

I am the freedom of your every whim

Who ignites the energy you breathe in?

Who allows your fertile soil to grow?

Who drives people to the edge of Reason?

I am the Pulse, I am the Rose

FIREFLY

The Firefly intensely glows

Her magic strong yet fleeting

Strikes through the night, a dazzling show

Illuminating meeting

So much that's taught, cannot be caught

Though powerful and brightening

Her freedom many folk have sought

A flash of passing lightning

We need her when our days are dark

To stoke our inner fire

For when she flies, she lights a spark

that can't fail to inspire

Compelling us our truth to show

as fast our hearts are beating

The Firefly intensely glows

Her magic strong yet fleeting

PLEASURE

Pleasure Seekers

Do what brings you joy in life, for this more joy returns

There's no need to be coy, this slice of time will quickly turn

Do what lights you up inside, reside in what ignites you

Take opinions in your stride, breathe into what excites you

Be who you are meant to be, exude your very essence

Then others soon content will be to linger in your presence

Be the spark and make your mark in ways that feel authentic

All limiting beliefs now park, make truth be your incentive

Conformity comes at a price, the more we live we learn

to do what brings us joy in life, for this more joy returns

WILD CHILD

Just because you packaged away

that rebellious red-head

and her tarty little leather skirt - don't think she left you!

She is still there wriggling beneath your sensible sweater, pulling at the hem of your just-right jeans

like a bitch on heat

She has longings, you know?

She wants to dangle from your ears like a frenzied chandelier

and ruffle up your ridiculous little bob until

it can no longer be recognised

She longs to pierce into your belly button and swagger your hips

and swing from your nipples

for the whole wide world to see!

You can try all you might to cage that crafty minx

but she'll scratch her nails down

your over-responsible back

if you don't respond to her

histrionics

Dance with her

and

she'll show you the way

Home.

Cobra

My energy doesn't FIT IN!

It bursts out like a restless fire stoked by the impulse of message

When I try to simmer down or appear more objective it blazes,

burning my bones and threatening to peak just for the sheer hell of it

My energy begs for my trust via the most dramatic of disturbances

for all explosions return us

to the heart

anyway

My energy is a powerhouse.

It rattles through my urgent hips, thrusting thirstily for more arousal

It curls through my feminine form like a cobra

writhing and hissing

luring me into its raspy root with an uncompromising conviction

For I am here to emit and express and submit

to that uncanny force much bigger than we know.

This crafty old snake of an energy shows me that my peace is found through the readiness of heat

and simply must be inhabited with all of

its fiery fullness

in order to fulfil

And who am I to argue with that sage of a serpent?

BUTTERFLY BLISS

As I reclined and closed my eyes

Breathed deep, released some body sighs

Feet on the ground with outstretched thighs

The trembling began to rise

It was euphoric, can't deny

To feel made love to by the sky

No need to do, no need to try

But open and be tantalised

My body rippled in wild waves

Received the love and in bliss bathed

Amazed by what this movement gave

What thrill to be divine love's slave

My yoni fluttered, pelvis rolled

Self-love expanded through this hold

My heart wide open and my soul

When we allow, so much unfolds

I moaned, I shook with ecstasy

And let joy's movements move through me

They played me instrumentally

Life force just wants us to be free

My body loved this huge surprise

Surrendering to paradise

Pulsating cells, revitalised

Enlivened by vibrations wise

Who knew what could emerge from here?

Such twinkling feelings did appear!

For source is palpable and near

We're loved, we're held, divinely steered

Joy Lines

There's no one that can steal your joy

This energy's a sacred toy

with which your soul can always play

No one can take your joy away

Your inner joy belongs to you

When you engage, the world can too

Does not depend on anything

or anyone to make it sing

There's no one that can make it wrong

It's there in days short and those long

It flirts with life, it's love's best friend

It is with joy these words are penned

How do you, your own source deploy?

For joy is the most sacred toy!

BACKSTACY

Deft hands swept like feathers

into sacred crooks of holding

Dusting away old stories and teasing the Life back through

Melting and swirling beneath your magical touch

In full surrender to my senses

It seemed to arrive from nowhere!

This ecstatic wave galloping through my vertebrae

like a wild palomino

charging in amorous abandon through

my sorceress spine

My head perplexed by the novelty of such a feeling

and my body oblivious to the limitations of reasoning

Writhing and convulsing

Shivering and shaking

Awake and aroused and illuminated

in a way I've

Never known before

PRESENT-ING

Life is precious

Life is short

You must step out

You must cavort

The bees will buzz

The flowers bloom

Do not spend your

whole life on Zoom

Float with the clouds

Dance with the breeze

Each breath a moment

We can seize

The years roll by

The cars rush past

We are not all

the shadows cast

Life is fragile

Life is now

Say yes although

you don't know how

Catch others, let

yourself be caught

Life is precious

Life is short

HIGH TIME

The twinkling is happening.

A vortex of magical momentum is spiralling through my entity and sending subtle explosions of healing joy into the cosmos.

And it feels good.

I did not plan for this or control this.

I did not get to decide when and how it happened.

It just did.

And the gratitude is galactic.

As I allow the rapturous ripples of resonance to vibrate within, I am

dumbfounded.

I deepen further into the timelessness of Trust with each incredible spark of universal affirmation.

Each foggy furlong of frustration formed a sacred part of this becoming

For there is no alchemy without awareness

and no transformation without courage.

We heal in our surrender

We reform in our patience

We flourish through our faith

And although it may seem illusive,

What we ask for is only a belief away.

Yes. You can!

Counterparts

The other side of grief

Is love beyond all measure

The other side of pain that's deep

Is pure and total pleasure

The other side of crying

Is joy in all its forms

The other side of sighing

Is taking life by storm

The other side of losing

Is unexpected gain

Perspective's for the choosing

We can #beginagain

The opposites connected

For everything is joined

By both we are affected

Two sides of the same coin

From doubting to belief

All held within our hearts

The other side of grief

Is love that's off the charts

Tula

Two soles pound the clay-like sand

Each thud echoing the grounded drum beat

Ankle chain charms chinking hypnotically

The clammy heat gleaming like bindis on her forehead

Her cheeks aglow with the fire of expression

This is the dance of creation.

What it is to harness the hungry strength of her spirit,

to stamp her soul into the thirsty earth!

They were waiting for her coming.

Now mesmerised by the dancing ribbons of her energy

Metamorphosing with each moment

Circles, squiggles and twists

Curving and spiralling towards the admiring stars

The flames of her aching loins powering each affirming step

Her wild passion flower heart aligned with the rugged beauty surrounding her

Beating to the calling of the cheering constellations

She has arrived.

And she trusts the calling of the universe. TULA!

ESSENCE

It is a tiny spinning seed of constant generation

When you've encountered it you've freed the source of your creation

So minuscule but don't be fooled, it sparks a flame ginormous

Do not by outer roles be ruled, pure energy works for us

It moved me so to feel the flow from whence my soul first started

Each time I let it move I flow, invention's open-hearted

There is not much to want or need when you've felt your vibration

When you've encountered it you've freed the source of your creation

Liberty

Don't have to please or be more measured

I have a right to my own pleasure

I'm female and I have my needs

When I am hungry, I shall feed

Don't have to temper lust or rage

The wilderness inside may rage

Won't simmer down or be subdued

Can love myself as much as you

There's darkness deep inside my womb

That lets the wild and free have room

That holds it all, no fear of night

My power centre is my right

I have a voice, I take a stance

I come from choice, I shake, I dance

I feel, I love, I am alive

I rise above, I take deep dives

Expressing myself at my leisure

I have a right to my own pleasure

Unlaced : Double Refrain Ballade

She came alive in dreams

her senses led the way

Unrivalled libertine

Make love to life today!

We're fifty shades of grey

The thrill is worth the chase

Yes, have your wicked way

Our bodies long to taste

No anti-ageing creams

could smooth her truth away

She soon ran out of means

Make love to life today!

Her soul cracked through the clay

Rough diamonds gleam with grace

Our minds lead us astray

Our bodies long to taste

She cried, she laughed, she screamed

She ate, she loved, she prayed

Who knows what all this means?

Make love to life today!

Move like a Mantaray

Unclasp that jewelled case

Let passion have its say

Our bodies long to taste

She smiled as her hips swayed

Make love to life today!

Alive are The Unlaced

Our bodies long to taste

ECSTATIC NUMBER

I am a conductor.

A conductor of a limitless symphony

that swings through my pelvis

and rings through my breasts

This music is momentous!

It is a music that charges through the stratosphere

in jubilant spontaneity

Each subtle trace of my nipple cascading the scales of ecstasy

and erupting

into helpless harmony

I am a conductor.

Yet somehow, my ensemble is carried

by an impishly pure energy

which guides

my every stroke

I am guided by ecstasy

and inspired by love

My clitoris throbs theatrically

just when the crescendo

is about to be reached

and I do so love

the thunder

of

an

instrumental

climax

WHILST YOU CAN

For pity's sake, stop being so relentlessly constructive, will you!

Kick off those well-worn moccasins-of-doing and let yourself relax.

Yes. Now.

You are allowed and this might come as some sort of a shock but:

You deserve it.

We were not created to be human Zoom-call-conductors.

We were not put on this Earth to pour our heart's energy into constant virtual contact or to spend our sacred existence craning our knackered necks over tiny, static screens

searching for the next desperate dopamine hit of external validation

We were not made to invest our souls in inconsequential meetings

or to waste our precious life force

planning the next time that we might

actually be available to experience some desperate morsel of

glimpsed happiness.

For that time is now, dear friend.

And there is so much pleasure available if you'd simply let your fidgety little fingers take a moment to feel it all!

There is a joy that bubbles at your source and it is begging you to express its innocence.

Each time you choose it, it spurts out of you like a flirtatious fountain

effervescing with attractive aliveness

and flowing you into even greater goodness.

Will you savour the juicy fruits of fun that flutter inside of your loins

when you prioritise

this very instant?

Go on. I dare you!

Starfish

Seashells on the seashore

The sand is warm and course

My lust for you leaves me raw

Together we're a force

Limbs and lips entwining

We crash like breaking waves

It's all in perfect timing

You're just the type I crave

Recall the rhythmic raining

Soft pattering, warm tin

With you there's no restraining

And you know I'm all in

You are a wild arouser

I don't want this to stop

And I'm no window browser

We move to Iggy Pop

My body will dehisce

You lead my mind astray

You said I was your starfish

Upon the Île de Ré

Explosive Flower

She is a radiant sunflower

Drinking in the dazzling juice of the universe in splendid surrender

Each impassioned imbibement projected into roaring red rays

Her aura surrounding me in a blindingly beautiful golden light

She is an undulating chasm of prosperity,

turning and yearning

and reaching far and wide into the endless boundaries of possibility

Spirit stretching through sensual stalk and passionate petal

Powerfully feminine

Wildly open

and avidly amorous

She moans and aches for her full shining

Each shivering orgasm like a blossoming bud of

self-actualisation

SELF-LOVE

Some Body

You're beautiful the way you are

Yes, with the lumps and bumps and scars

With all the crow's feet and the wrinkles

The hairs gone grey, the teenage pimples

You're beautiful, nothing to change

Must not your own face rearrange

It tells a tale of stories lived

The way you are has much to give

The moles, the blemishes, the frizz

All part of what a real life is

The love handles and cellulite

Want your acceptance - yes, that's right!

Imperfect, quirky - that's the norm

Let's celebrate our human form

The natural you will take you far

You're beautiful the way you are

SANCTITY

Returning to the place within

will always bring you home

It stays with you through thick and thin

wherever your soul roams

Inside yourself you can confide

There is a source maternal

To pull in doesn't mean to hide

Your soul voice is eternal

Attuning to your centred place

Communing with your wisdom

You'll find a source of natural grace

And you'll have more to give them

We can fill back up to the brim

A skill we all can hone

Returning to the place within

will always bring you home

Self-Love

Self-love is not a selfish choice

It's not all me me me

It is a soft, survival voice

That tells us what we need

Self-love is a necessity

Despite some folks' conviction

It's treating yourself carefully

It frees you from addiction

Self-love is not an ego thing

Not for the self-obsessed

It knows we can't do everything

And helps us do what's best

Self-love can heal the deepest scars

And calm our inner racket

Its reputation somewhat marred

By those who often lack it

It is the dew upon the weeds

A very human thirst

To help another that's in need

We must help ourselves first

Self-love's an act of bravery

It's honouring who we are

It's freedom from self-slavery

It is a guiding star

Enough

I am enough, I'm there for me

I love myself wholeheartedly

The shadows, skeletons and ghosts

The parts where I shine out the most

I am enough, I must not try

To prove myself through others' eyes

My struggles, setbacks and my glory

They're all a part of a bigger story

I am enough, yes come what may

When I rise up, when I'm astray

I hold myself in full permission

Acceptance is my only mission

I am enough, have been since birth

I do not have to prove my worth

In failure and in my success

I am enough, no more, no less

I'm not their viewpoints or suggestions

My value's never been in question

I must not pass approval's test

I matter at my worst and best

Whether they smile or disagree

I am enough, I'm there for me

and through God's eyes myself I see

I love myself wholeheartedly

The Waters Within

Surrendered limbs sift through the reeds

lulling stubborn thought loops into

acquiescence

There is nothing to meet my resistance

other than the constant caress

of fluidity

My mind seeks to fight the flow with its contrived agendas

Yet the weightless gyrations send me into a softer power

Taught tears begin to loosen, pouring through despite themselves

Feelers must surrender,

counsel the subtle circles of the wise water

I am a passenger

on a lonely lake

and when I meet myself here

My Wildheart heart breathes,

buoyantly melancholic

forgiving as the restless rhythm of the rippling reeds

SELF-LOVE AFFAIR

There is a time for no one else

A time to fall into yourself

when you are held by your own weight

and you become your own soul mate

A time to catch yourself full on

To be the friend you can land on

To soften and yourself to hold

To let a deep self-love unfold

There is a time, the time is here

To feel your pain, to face your fears

whilst knowing that whatever comes

You're sheltered by a faithful one

who knows you inside out and still

will be there for you right until

You finally see your inner wealth

You've fallen for your own damn self

As We Are

No matter what, the fir trees stand

Their worth does not need proving

Majestic, verdant, tall and grand

No man their edge is smoothing

No matter what, the swallows swoop

Their ups and downs accepted

They do not have to jump through hoops

Pure freedom quite expected

No matter what, the wild palm shakes

Its gentle rhythm easy

You feel the pulsing that it makes

Seducing yet not sleazy

No matter what, we too are here

Belonging without question

When we slow down it all seems clear

We hear the Earth's suggestions

For we're the rocks, the shoots, the ground

The sky, the sun, the spaces

Embrace your place, make your own sounds

We're mirrors of God's graces

Now finally I understand

What lands when we stop moving

No matter what, the fir trees stand

Their worth does not need proving

All to Love

Don't ever doubt the joy you bring

Your soul, a many-splendored thing

The way you are, the way you speak

By definition quite unique

Don't ever underestimate

Your value always highly rate

For you are special and much needed

Despite how you might have been treated

Don't ever think that you are less

Your beauty is your humanness

When everything feels topsy-turvy

You're loveable and you are worthy

The person who you are innately

offers much and matters greatly

You are cherished, you are treasured

You are loved beyond all measure

You're not alone when suffering

Your soul, a truly splendid thing

Love Anyway

Love, no matter what they say

Love twice as much, love anyway

It doesn't serve to hold a grudge

Expand your heart, accept and budge!

Love with everything you've got

Love wholly, don't blow cold and hot

Love all that's there, although it's hard

Embrace it all, do not discard

Love when others disappear

It's all that counts, it's why we fear

For when we love ourselves like this

Then others too receive our bliss

So, love no matter what they say

Love twice as much, love anyway

Ageing Gracefully

With age the layers fall away, there's grace in what we're shedding

With every single hair gone grey, much wisdom is embedding

What used to be a travesty can now be viewed with kindness

From wholeness life now we can see, without that youthful blindness

With age we've known all kinds of rage, the sage in us more present

Although the inner wars still wage, attachment to them lessens

We feel less need to perform deeds because that's what's expected

Authentic presence supersedes, from inside we're connected

With age we realise who has stayed with us and where our home is

We've worked out who we truly trust, we know it's time to own this

Acceptance, patience, loyalty and feelings soft and tender

Are what gives our life quality, less fight and more surrender

With age life does not become beige, the colours rich and gentle

Companionship weaves through this phase, a love less temperamental

We've come back home, no more astray, upon strong ground we're treading

With age the layers fall away, there's grace in what we're shedding

The Garden of my Higher Self

There is a garden far beyond

Where bamboo shoots surround a pond

Secluded, lush and turquoise green

A place where only I have been

Where dragonflies vibrate close by

I take deep breaths and close my eyes

Imbibing nature's amber nectar

Miles away from life's conjecture

In the distance crickets buzz

Cool moss beneath my feet like fuzz

Soft and sensual, summer rug

I give myself a tender hug

The glistening surface of the pond

Mirroring my natural bond

With all the thriving stems and shoots

Some swallows pass, an owl hoots

Willows like a horse's mane

Cascade with tears of joy, no pain

And butterflies of cornflower blue

Flash past to tell me, just be you

This is a garden where I know

The beauty of my soul can glow

Its pond shines rich with nature's wealth

The garden of my higher self

Arrival

What will it take for you to finally get into your numb little skull that -

You're already THERE?

Yes, right there - the exact spot in which you are currently standing

is THE place

for which you were intended.

But I'm not yet rich?

Or famous?

Or skinny?

Or successful?

I hear you say.

I haven't bought a house

got married

had children

owned a cockatiel

bought a camper van

or eloped to Outer Mongolia...

I am not as clever/funny/artistic/inspiring/confident as....(insert a friend's name here)

For Goodness sake!

Maybe you will one day. And maybe you won't ever be.

And your hypotheses and comparisons are all beside the point quite frankly.

For the point is that RIGHT NOW

is your destiny

The precise instant in which you gaze your forgivably cynical eyes upon this text

is YOUR MOMENT!

Do you feel the Spring breeze skipping across your sacred cheeks?

Do you hear the birds wolf-whistling at your beautifully imperfect human soul?

Can you feel the invigorating whoosh of your Heart's Falls as you surge beyond the most ruthless of rocks?

The charging forth of your undeniable, vulnerable magnificence

You are loved, do you know that?

Loved, needed, held, desired and cherished much more than you may ever even realise.

Unless, of course, you choose to pause for a millisecond and catch your glory

in the cool mirroring of the

river's revelation

one miraculously sunny afternoon

and let yourself

be

clearly

seen

Yes! There you are.

Thank you for finally

showing up!

Forest Bathing

Deep within the forest arms self-love finds its expression

Comparisons all fade away as does the soul's suppression

There's freedom here, fresh signs appear, I open to what's calling

A greater sense of truth is near, into its trust I'm falling

Deep within the forest's heart the birdsong offers choices

We cannot hear ourselves until we silence social voices

What others think is their spilled ink, the mystery's universal

We're full of kinks, our hearts still pink, this is no dress rehearsal

The great outdoors opens my pores, untwists where there's compression

Deep within the forest arms self-love finds its expression

LOVE

So much Love

There's love that cries from bluebird skies

There's love when days are hazy

It is a power that defies

There's love amidst the crazy

There's love when you feel most alone

It's there and it surrounds you

There's love transmitted through your phone

When circumstance house-bounds you

There's love and it is there for you

It's free and for the sourcing

We all need it to make it through

Reach out and it starts coursing

Yes, may it pour from bluebird skies

Abundance, be our weather

There's so much love for you and I

I feel it more than ever

Messy Love

Love is messy, get stuck in

Sometimes you lose, sometimes you win

Can be electric, can be slow

Into a spin your heart it throws

Love is messy, love is rough

It's tender, gentle, fierce and tough

Seduces you and beckons sweetly

Love can change your life completely

Love can burn and love can heal

It makes you moan, it makes you squeal

and all the colours come alive

Love lights you up, love helps you thrive

Love is precious, love's intense

Confusing yet makes perfect sense

It's clumsy and it's full of grace

It's painted over your whole face

More powerful than we can know

Not always tied up with a bow

You long for it when it has gone

Love is messy, bring it on

LOVE IS

Love's the answer, love's the choice

Love's the most supportive voice

Love's the action, love's the clue

Don't hold back, say "I love you"

Love's the power, love's the win

May love your gestures underpin

Love's the beauty, love's what mends

Love's wide open, love defends

Love's the reason, love prevails

Be love's container on life's trail

Love's far brighter than our doubts

Drink it in and ooze it out

Love says you will find a way

Love's the answer, every day

Humility

Humility's the knowing there is much I do not know

Humility is gratitude and going with the flow

Humility is bowing to my perfect imperfection

Humility is showing who I am, it's true connection

Humility is doing what I can with love and grace

Humility's great reverence for nature's healing space

Humility is openness, the willingness to change

Humility accepts that which my mind cannot explain

Humility is tolerance, allowances and faith

It's noticing I'm fortunate when I am warm and safe

Each circumstance is showing me more ways that I can grow

Humility's the knowing there is much I do not know

Quantum Entanglement

Distance means nothing

When it comes to this kind of connection

Where my every breath is felt like the soft mist on an eternal autumn garden

Where my needs are heard intuitively through rainbows and rivers

and met with love and loyalty

No, we do not need the usual social mannerisms

that squash and placate and

urge with their false promise of

security

With you, my heavy heart is held and known in intimate detail,

cocooned in a cradle of infinite love

We blend effortlessly

without the proximity of space or time to corrupt or confine

Together magically manifesting soul synchronicity

in dreamlike dance and knowing silence

A mirror that knows me better than I know myself

Reflecting unseen parts through symbiotic sensing

Sometimes the mind pines for the normality of real-time reassurance

But we are beyond all that.

Midnight Message

Last night I had a dream in which I knew of my brightness but could not fully see it.

A dream in which I needed to awaken for an important event of which the significance had not yet been revealed to me.

Eventually I actually physically woke up, ridiculously thirsty, and drank a cool ginger beer in passionate rapidity.

It was pleasant and yet did not even touch the sides!

I am so thirsty in so many ways these days that I wonder; Could I ever be completely quenched?

What I do know now though, is that you cannot 'have' the kind of love that I am currently experiencing.

It is a love that **just is** and therefore exists of its own accord without the need for possession or identical reciprocation.

This love does not depend on another and yet sometimes clings to human souls

so that it may be made tangible to

The Outside World.

It can be frustrating for the well-meaning mind to accept and believe that which it cannot explain.

Bewildering to lack words to quantify that which the soul knows so deeply.

Intense to experience a love this dazzling.

And yet so very beautiful.

Faithful Father

You beam out from the sleepy trees

Fresh faced and good intention

I'm bolstered by your energy

Your love and your attention

Perching like the blackbird flock

in silent observation

Your memories so much unlock

For you, pure adoration

The softness of the grazing sheep

The innocence of morning

Bring back a love that runs so deep

eternal and adorning

You stand beside me, this I know

I hear words of affection

Go gentle, tender, kind and slow

my love, you've my protection

Articulation

Tell the people in your life just what they mean to you

No holding back now, rise above, what would love have you do?

The items bought, the titles sought, are not what gives life meaning

The ones that by your side have fought deserve your love's live-streaming

Speak out the words, your heart is heard, they'll be received with pleasure

To speak the truth is not absurd, confess what you most treasure

What you divulge, returns for sure, it's love that gets us through

Tell the people in your life just what they mean to you

The Real Deal

True love doesn't leave you hanging on for any morsel of reciprocation that might pacify your starving heart.

It doesn't keep you haplessly waiting for a non-committal text message or leave you feasting on a maybe like a destitute devotee.

It doesn't beg

or brag

or bend-over-backwards for belonging

because it knows its own worth in the humblest of ways.

True love is an apple.

A rosy-red Braeburn that blushes with beauty

and bursts with natural flavour.

It is sweet

and bold

and spicy

and delicious

and it shines so naturally that the whole world wants to come and take a bite.

True love is gentle

and respectful

it is harmless

harmonious

imperfect

and hopeful.

True love is patient and forgiving

and it holds us

like a deckchair

as we ease back into

the relaxed version of ourselves

that we always wanted to be.

True love laughs

and lasts

and let's you know that it's there.

And the funny thing is

It always has been

It's just that we can't see it

until we choose to

Vibrant Females

Vibrant females change the world

their colours multi-shaded

Creating from whatever's hurled

their way, not tired or jaded

Vibrant females own their space

light up the path for others

They're passionate and full of grace

Their face shows they're life-lovers

Vibrant females lead with fun

They're playful, deep, creative

They know the way to get things done

Courageous, real, persuasive

They serve from heart, they play the part

the universe intended

When things go wrong, they set restart

Resurface strong and mended

They're lovers, laughers, fierce yet girls

Their life force you can't fade it

Vibrant females change the world

their colours multi-shaded

Grandma's Girl

Swirling ears like seashore shells

Piano playing fingers

You loved me so much, I could tell

Your tenderness still lingers

Saturdays you'd come and stay

I'd lay upon you, dreaming

Now don't be getting idol, nay!

Your wise blue eyes said, gleaming

We wrote and wrote, you kept my notes

You travelled without moving

Italian squares and castle moats

The intrigue and the new things

You always wished me safe and well

No rose glasses, no blinkers

You loved me so much, I could tell

Your tenderness still lingers

Breakers

It was the one that broke over your head like

a freshly cracked egg

that caused the most amusement

All the more so given the succession of sideward breakers

that slammed you back into the ocean's belly

offering little chance of recovery

Such a good sport

All hedgehog-haired and smiley-eyed

Even your much-worn sunglasses rolled into the surf

engulfed forever in Spanish swell

We walked hand-in-hand along the ballooning bay

Feet tickled by the aftermath of foamed festoon

What takes us back to childhood is always a winner.

INEVITABLE

There's nothing you can DO about

being in love

You just ARE

And that's it.

You can try all you like to shelve it

to push it away

to get over it...

but it just won't work.

You can even try to hang your hopelessly loved-up little heart in the back of your winter wardrobe, deluding yourself that it will be disguised by all of your new-fangled seasonal purchases

But you are a fool, let's face it!

Nothing but a wide-eyed smitten kitten!

You, dear friend, have been struck by an enigmatic force far greater than anything your willpower alone can fight against.

Love cannot be denied

or disguised

or defied

Love bowls you over

and knocks you for six

and sends you head over heels

Love hurts

and heals

and hopes

and happens quite unexpectedly half the time

and that's the whole crazy, ridiculous

point of it

so

all you can DO is to

Let it BE

Electric Guitar

You had a love of learning

I guess it kept you young

A thirst that kept on burning

A passion you passed on

No cynicism in you

No tired, tested looks

When you were ill and thin you

still opened that new book

It was a lifelong mission

upon your bucket list

When you were in remission

No way this chance you'd miss

You sounded animated

A kid with a new toy

Not fair your time was fated

But you played on with joy

When I returned that morning

The shock was hard to take

I wish I'd had some warning

You looked like you might break

A skeleton so hollow

I broke before your eyes

But you still strummed and followed

those happy notes, with pride

It hurt to see your suffering

You made me sing along

Could hardly stop from blubbering

But your thin hands played on

A shiny red electric

A sixties-sounding twang

To hell with all the sceptics

You strummed away, I sang

In me you have awoken

The will to see things through

Your body it was broken

But how you spirit flew

Belonging

To be shown how to love gently and kindly and selflessly

is no small thing.

Love poured from your lips in affirming words, helpful thoughts and open guidance.

Love teamed through your considerate gestures, your inclusive humour and your unfailing generosity.

Each time that I returned home, you greeted me with childlike joy, squeezing me with a unique enthusiasm that was beyond comparison.

Your love made me feel;

loveable

special

magical

protected

invincible

normal

You spent willing hours choosing walking routes and cute country pubs in which to spend our precious hours.

You wanted to spend time with me. To share memories with me. To find out about me. To know me.

You loved me unconditionally. Regardless.

With open arms.

Your love flows on like a timeless poem

in my eccentric little heart.

And however out-of-the-box I am,

with you I will always

Belong

Forwards

The miles that you've walked by side

The times that we've both witnessed

We find our rhythm with each stride

I'm blessed to have you in this

Still with me when our dreams divert

Drift back with each step taken

You've walked with me through loss and hurt

My rock when I feel shaken

My family, my sense of place

My home and my companion

Sometimes we can't align our pace

But you're my deep Grand Canyon

I'm grateful for the landscapes wide

The skies that we've both weathered

It's when we walk, that you confide

We see so much together

When you are strolling by my side

I could walk on forever

STRONG-HEARTED WOMEN

Strong-hearted women

A bond that is unspoken

I put my trust into them

Lean in when I feel broken

No jealousy or bitching

We raise each other's game

There's no need for self-pitching

There's no need to explain

A fellowship of feelers

A code that can't be cracked

Support each other's healing

With dignity and tact

One look and I feel understood

We're not in competition

In gratitude of womanhood

Of female intuition

Loyalty

I believe in you and our relationship and

I always will.

My heart remembers everything that you have done to love and support me.

Yes. Even when we fight.

I stand up for you. I stand up for us. And we are a united front. And we have each other's backs.

I care how you feel. I care how I make you feel. And I seek to show this through my words and actions.

We are an ever-evolving journey and I am open and curious about our becoming.

When there is physical or emotional distance, there is trust. Trust that we'll come back. That we'll reconnect. And that this space was needed.

I am big enough to say sorry when I mess up. And I will. Repeatedly.

We laugh. We cry. We celebrate. We commiserate. And we know that we can always be ourselves together whilst being held

In total acceptance.

When you ask me for help I will respond. In the best way that I can. With a willing heart.

I speak highly of you to others.

Loyalty

KEEPER

You stayed when all the chips were down

Leaned in and loved me deeper

When things got tough you stayed around

That's why you are a keeper

You've stayed though we have our own ways

and you don't always get me

Supporting me throughout my days

Each time I grow, you let me

You've stayed through lightness and in shade

In loyalty, in freedom

And such a peaceful home you've made

Your earthy tones, I need them

I am the fire, you're the ground

We are each other's teachers

When things got tough you stayed around

That's why you are a keeper

Soul Sherpa

You stood with me in trauma

In doubt and in despair

The coldness felt much warmer

When you were standing there

You stood with me in power

In knowingness, in growth

There in changing hours

When I needed you the most

You stood there in anxiety

Fragility and strength

Boldly, softly, quietly

Can't say how much this meant

You stood with me through thick and thin

No judgement, full attention

You helped cut through the background din

I clarified intentions

I put my trust there on the line

You stood there, steadfastly

Our meeting perfectly aligned

For it was meant to be

In-to-me-see

It's in the knowing glances

It's in the listening ears

It's in the crazy dances

It's just you being here

It's in the reassurance

The cuddles and the touch

In patience and endurance

I value you so much

It's in the subtle asking

The love behind-the-scenes

To be with you's like basking

In sunny, soulful dreams

It's in the compensation

The bolstering, the care

The mutual celebration

The calling forth, the shares

I can't do this without you

You mean the world to me

I never have to doubt you

For you in-to-me-see

Heartily

The heart is where we hold our truth

It goes wherever we go

To try to hold it back, no use

It's stronger than our ego

The heart contains our spirit's map

The journey often winding

When we take off our thinking cap

The heart's voice is spellbinding

It is not fooled by empty words

It sees right through pretending

We feel on purpose when it's stirred

Its power is unending

It has a world of love to give

It seeks not to be right

The heart is where our purpose lives

May you emit its light

Radiance

This afternoon the sunshine drenched our paths in the kindliest of ways.

As we ascended that good old winding route towards the faithful forest, we were blessed.

That splendid sun smiled on us with such eagerness that it made me feel the sacredness of our friendship on another scale entirely. It was almost as if the precious bond that we have formed was being affirmed by the weather Gods beaming down in joyful appreciation.

Or at least that's how it felt to me.

What I love about us is the ease in which

we slip into the language of the soul.

We do not waste time with empty exchange and superficial social pleasantries

Instead we dive into the goldmine of spontaneous insights which emerge from the ether when we only give them half a chance.

With you I can share from within and beyond. I can speak from what's there and

allude to the subtleties without the slightest need to translate.

What a gift it is, to have such a meaningful friendship

Be**YOU**tiful

When I was a skinny, spotty teenager walking down the stairs in my glaring green prom dress, my Dad told me that I looked beautiful. And he meant it. For in his eyes I was beautiful no matter what.

I feel so utterly blessed to have been loved by a Father who taught me that beauty is only skin deep. I was raised to know that my energy and actions are what define me and that the way I hold myself and relate to others is what makes me truly attractive.

Don't get me wrong, it is important to feel good about the way we look. To express our personality through our unique choice of clothes, accessories and outward appearance. And for many people looking good is a big and vital part of self-care.

But it is not the be-all and end-all.

We do not need to conform to the norms of air-brushed beauty imposed by social media to be beautiful.

We have not been given this precious time on earth to spend trying to change ourselves in order to be more beautiful.

Here's to the faces that show their laughter, their tears, their rage and their kindness.

Here's to the loveable eccentricity of our many shapes and forms.

Here's to the beauty of our imperfection

To be human is to be beautiful.

Thank you dear Dad, yet again...

LIVE POETRY

Would you like to experience some of my live poetry recitals?

By accessing this QR Code you gain exclusive access to a brand-new collection of live poetry videos in which you will discover more expressions of the wild, feminine spirit.

CONTENT WARNING: One of the videos contains profanity which may be offensive to some viewers and/or inappropriate for children. Viewer discretion is advised.

MORE ABOUT ME

When I lost my dear Dad to pancreatic cancer back in December 2015 it felt like my world had ended. Dad was my hero, my cheerleader and the most loyal, stable and loving presence in my life. On walking to work one bitterly cold winter morning back here in Switzerland after Dad's funeral, I was overcome with grief, sadness and anxiety. That morning I was seriously wondering how on earth I would manage to process all of these dramatic feelings and still get through my teaching day.

And then I received a message; "Write it down."

It was such timely and direct guidance that I simply had to honour it. As my freezing fingertips began furiously tapping into my iPhone, I noticed that the words were becoming poems that were almost writing themselves before my very eyes. There was a therapeutic process happening that would help me to deal with the intensity of my experience. From this very moment, the fire of my creativity would become a force that would evolve my soul beyond measure.

Since receiving this message, I have written every single day. Writing helps me to know, express and heal myself in ways which continue to thrill me. I share a poem every weekday on my blog and I can often be found reciting my poetry live on social media.

As well as being a passionate Poetess, Creative Leadership Coach and Facilitator, I am :

- an Aries woman, through and through.
- a highly-sensitive, highly-intuitive, high thrill-seeking being
- a self-confessed Crazy Cat Lady!
- an enthusiastic hobby jogger
- most alight when I am communing with nature in the forest.
- a Tantrika
- an Enneagram #4
- scared of lifts
- a fan of weird leggings
- on a life-long journey towards even greater self-love and self-expression.

Are you curious to explore your wild, feminine spirit in a personalised coaching experience with me?

Email me: samallencoachingcreatively@gmail.com

Find out more about what I do here:
www.samallencoachingcreatively.com

To hear more of my poetry, follow me on Insight Timer:

https://insig.ht/E4DFyJyUzfb

And connect with me on Facebook here:

www.facebook.com/samallencreativecoach/

BEFORE YOU GO

If you enjoyed this book or found it useful I'd be very grateful if you'd post a short review on Amazon. Your support really does make a difference and I read all the reviews personally so I can get your feedback and make this book even better.

If you'd like to leave a review then all you need to do is click the review link on this book's page on Amazon.

Printed in Great Britain
by Amazon

Eliza

The Millwright's daughter

Anne Mason